DOCTOR WATSON ARCHITECTS

INCOMPLETE WORKS
Volume One

VICTORIA WATSON

CONTENTS

Introduction

This book documents the work of a conceptual architectural practice called Doctor Watson Architects (DWA). Unlike professional architects, who earn their living by managing the design of buildings, DWA earns theirs by other means, connected to the design of buildings but not strictly speaking a form of professional architecture. For DWA, making architecture is a leisure activity, a hobby, a self-therapy, a means of relaxation after work, or on a Sunday.

And yet DWA are not without architectural ambition, quite to the contrary. DWA want to inscribe their practice in architectural history, to find a spatial language corresponding to the face of the times in which they live. It is this ambition that has led to their turning away from professional practice to locate what they do in the utopian space of universal architectural history. As a by-product of their struggles to produce and inhabit such a world, DWA have invented a new material medium, they call it AIR Grid.

Living right in the centre of London, DWA often experience places that are jam-packed full of activity during the daytime and completely abandoned at night (figure 01). The bifurcation is curiously exhilarating, because it is never clear which is more real, the intense daytime activity or the silent abandon of night. Not so long ago, DWA tried to capture the truth of the city in which they live in an artwork and, because they were trained in architecture, they turned to the medium with which they were most familiar: architectural drawing and model making, which is what led them to the discovery of AIR Grid.

DWA had first encountered the grid-form while working for professional architects. This key formative experience occurred during a 'year-out' working for a commercial architectural design practice called Gollins Melvin Ward (GMW). These architects were working on the design of a brand new office building, sited on the Strand in London, the client was Mobile Oil. DWA's year-out commenced as the Mobil Oil office building was nearing completion, they joined GMW's architectural team as the practice began work on a set of 'as-built' drawings.

Figure 01
St John's Square, Clerkenwell, Night View

The production of as-built drawings requires a considerable amount of time. It is a kind of mapping, whereby the original design drawings are related to the spatial relationships of the building, as it has actually been built (in effect the architects survey and draw the brand new building). The medium that interfaces between the original drawings and the as-built drawings is a rectilinear grid, which repeats at each floor-level of the building. The grid is treated as something immutable, while the actual elements of the building, whose location it determines, are treated as if they had somehow drifted from their intended to their as-built positions. By working on as-built drawings, DWA quickly realised the importance of the grid to the professional practice of architecture, because it is the one thing that can survive both the destruction of the drawing and of the building.

Fascinated by their discovery, DWA eventually came to the conclusion: the rectilinear grid is to modern architecture as Kazimir Malevich's Black Square is to modern painting, i.e., the point zero through which architects must pass if they want to escape the presuppositions of the capitalist world economy in which they work (figure 02). For DWA, conceiving and producing AIR Grid became a means of doing just that, eventually leading to the rejection of all formal criteria of professional architecture and the social demands connected with it.

As they started to work with AIR Grid, DWA began to notice how one modernist avant-garde architect, Ludwig Mies van der Rohe, had already gone some way toward releasing the grid from its captivity by professional practice. For that reason, the early days of DWA's unprofessional practice was preoccupied with a structured study of Miesian architecture (for more about this study see the postdoctoral thesis by Victoria Watson: /Atmosphere/ The Origin of Air Grid, published by Air Grid Publications in 2018).

DWA speculated: Mies, when he emigrated to America, became infected by two things. First, by the experience of his work, exhibited in New York's Museum of Modern Art and published as the subject of a book. The show and book were curated and written, respectively, by Philip Johnson, the book is still in print today: it is entitled Mies van der Rohe and was first published by the New York Museum of Modern Art in 1947. Second, Mies experienced

the grid as an organising principle of American cities.

Because he was able to identify with, rather than resist, his American infections, Mies began to use architecture as a means of exhibiting grids. And, thanks to his emphasis on the non-objective form of the grid, Mies' American buildings always stand out in their environing context. Mies buildings have an ambiguous relationship to their setting, appearing to hang there, in space, present but barely perceptible.

Figure 02
Kazimir Malevich, Black Square, detail, with cracks

Firsts

To begin with, DWA made two AIR Grid structures, it is hard to remember which one came first, they appeared sometime around 1999. They weren't very big and neither were they very heavy, the largest measured somewhere in the order of 21 x 21 x 33 centimetres and weighed about 50 grams. The support armature was made from white foam-board, 5 millimetres thick, which meant the smaller Grid looked too bulky for the delicate lattice body nested inside. The support armature was lined with small sheets of coloured paper, cut to size and marked with the order of the grid. The marked sheets were then glued in place, so as to establish the spatial locations of the pin-holes. The smaller Grid had a red lining, which set-off the metallic gold lattice very nicely. The blue colour of the larger Grid complimented the shiny, viscose, orange lattice body on the inside. Since then, the small, red and gold Grid has come to be known as Ochenrada, the larger, blue and orange Grid as Ochenrad.

It isn't clear what inspired DWA to make these first AIR Grids, one possible explanation is suggested by looking at Malevich's sketch *Suprematist Elements in Space, motif 1915* (figure 03). As you can see, Malevich drew four prisms, apparently floating in space. Perhaps the first AIR Grid structures were speculations about what you might expect to find inside one of those prisms!

Malevich's Suprematist drawings and paintings had sometimes encouraged his students to think about space as a means of interplanetary travel. Ochenrada and Ochenrad prompted the same feelings in DWA, they dreamt of leaving the Earth and of drifting, like space-junk, amidst the planets, moons and stars.

References:
Kazimir **Malevich**, *The Non-Objective World, The Manifesto of Suprematism,* Dover Publications, INC, Mineola New York, 2003
Andrei **Nakov**, *Malevich, Volume 3, Painting the Absolute,* Lund Humphries, Farnham & Burlington, 2010

Figure 03
Kazimir Malevich, Suprematist Elements in Space, motif 1915, version 1927.* This drawing was reproduced in Malevich's book Die Gegenstandlose Welt, published in Germany in 1927 as volume 11 of the series of Bauhaus books. It was not until 1959 that a version of the book was published in English, it was called The Non-Objective World. The translation was based on the German version, because in those days the Russian version was unavailable.**

* Nakov, 2010, 77
** Malevich, 2003, 9

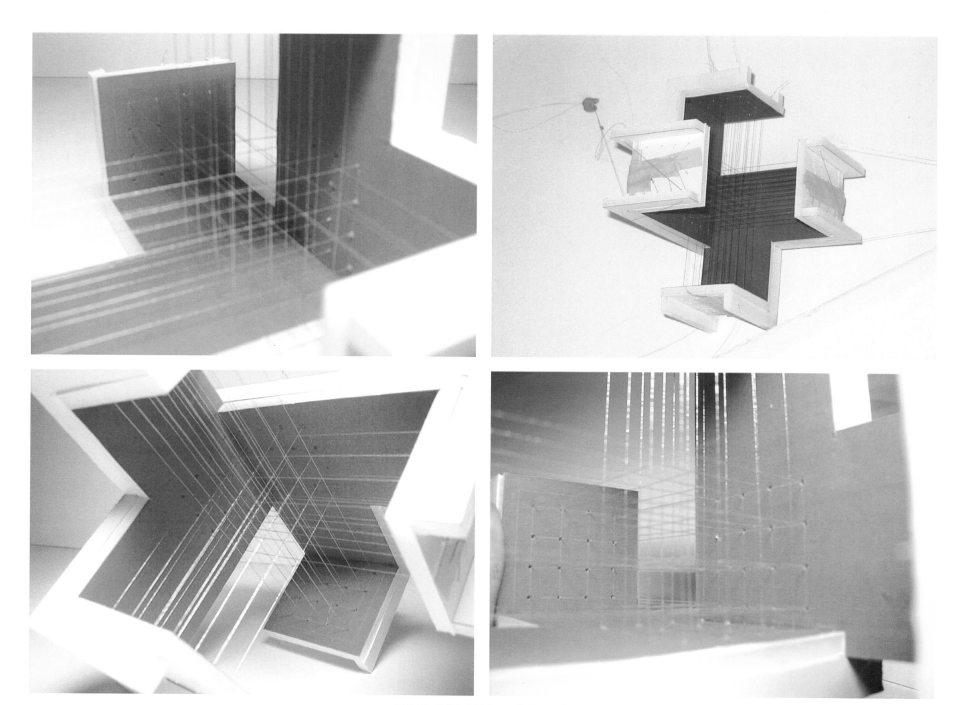

OCHENRADA, 4 VIEWS

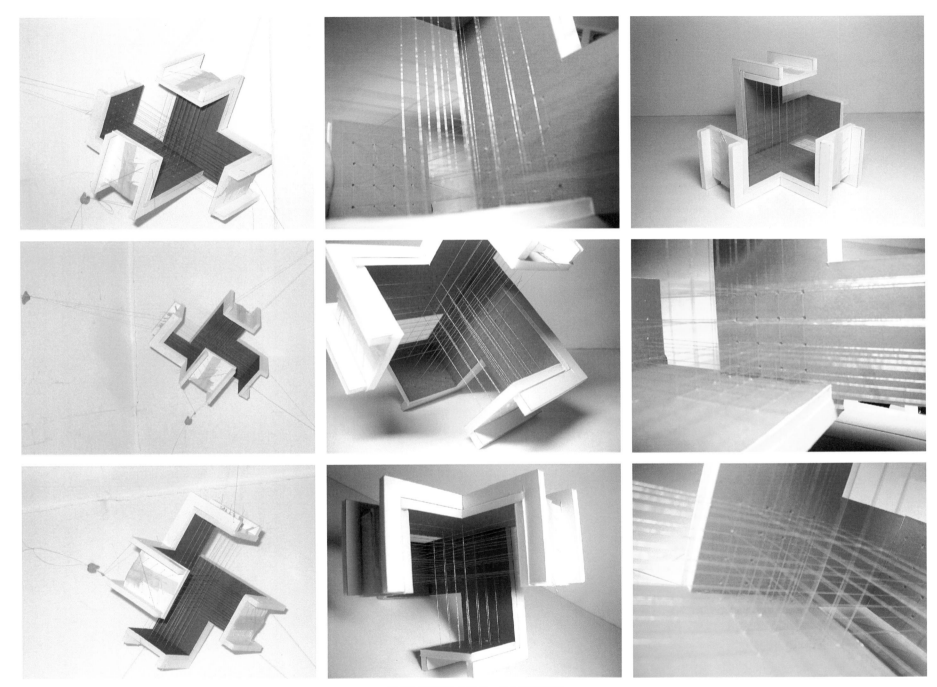

OCHENRADA, 9 VIEWS

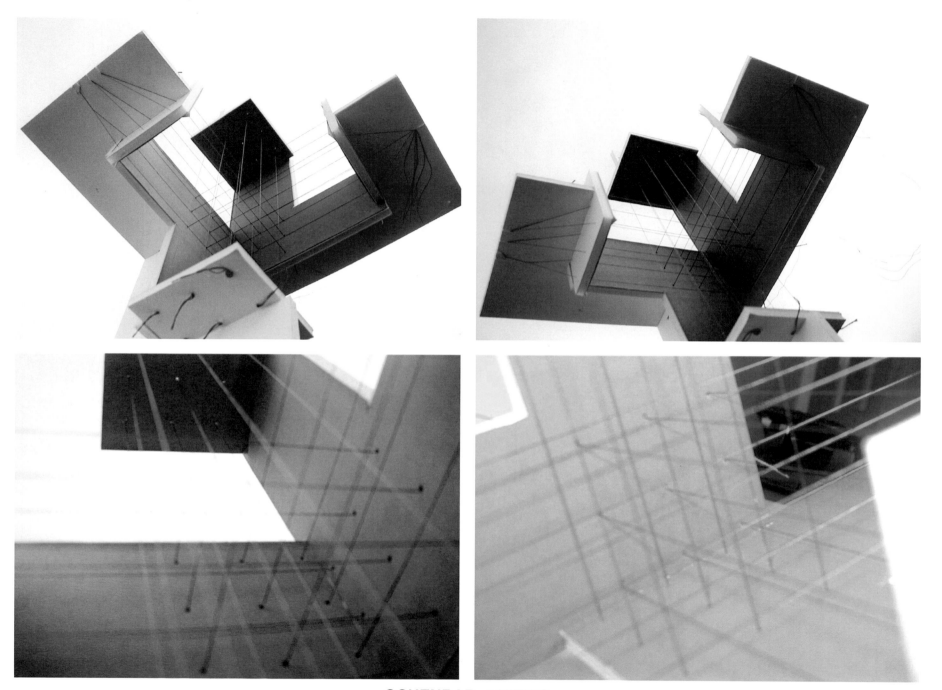

OCHENRAD, 4 VIEWS

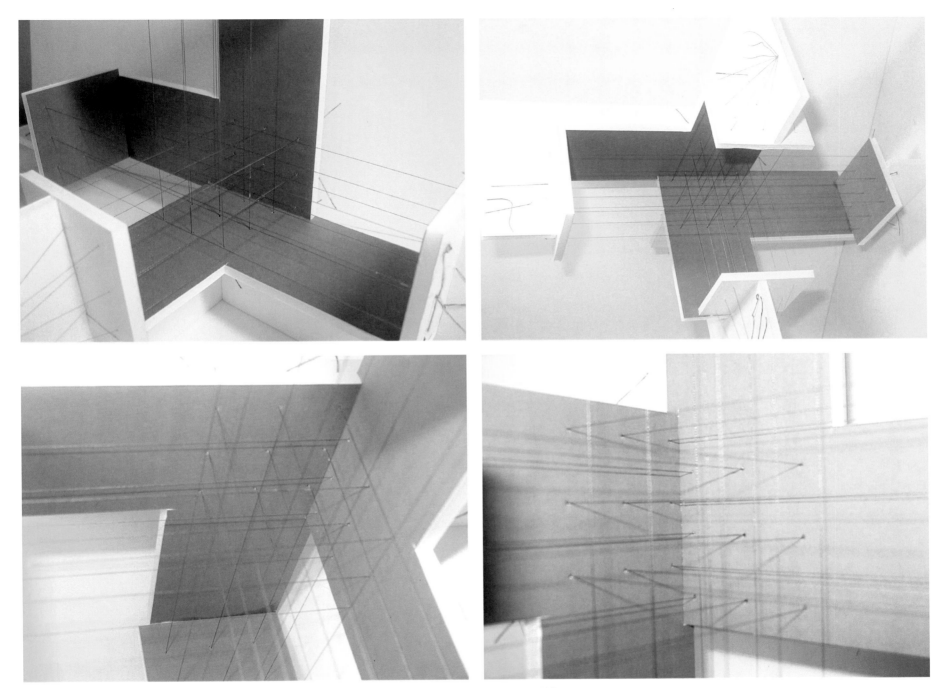

OCHENRAD, 4 VIEWS

Lake Shore

The first AIR Grid to be modelled on a Miesian building was a study of the twinned apartment blocks, nos. 860-880 Lake Shore Drive, Chicago 1948-'51. When they first saw them, DWA were struck by the way the twins appeared to be weightless, as if they were hanging in the air, hovering but not quite touching the ground. They were reminded of some remarks made by Malevich about the difference between the engineer and the architect. In his essay entitled *1/48 The World as Non-Objectivity*, Malevich wrote:

(O)nly one difference exists between them: the first forms an object as something 'concrete,' the second as something 'non-objective,' and something 'derived,' therefore there is no right of appeal against the decisions of the second; in the case of the first, one can appeal to consciousness, to reason, to calculation; the second distributes weight in an artistic shape or form, the first in utilitarian necessity of the object; the second is always comfortable, the first is never comfortable...(p282)

It seemed to DWA, the gravity/building relationship of Lake Shore Drive was far more 'non-objective' than it was 'concrete.' They tried to learn a little more about what Malevich meant by non-objective. In casting around for clues, they came across the thought of the highly influential philosopher Arthur Schopenhauer and were struck by his discussions of gravity, materiality and mind in the sections on architecture in his *The World as Will and Representation* (see volume 1, book three, §43 & volume 2 chapter XXXV).

Mies and Malevich met in Berlin in 1927, there is little record of what they said to one another but according to Nakov (2010, 69-70) Malevich talked about the link between his three-dimensional works, known as 'architectons' and Gothic architecture.

References:

Kazimir **Malevich**, *The World as Non-Objectivity, unpublished writings, 1922-25, Vol. III*, Troels Anderson (ed), Borgen, Copenhagen, 1976

Arthur **Schopenhauer**, *The World as Will and Representation, volume 1 & volume 2*, E.F.J Payne (trans), Dover Publications, Inc, New York, 1958

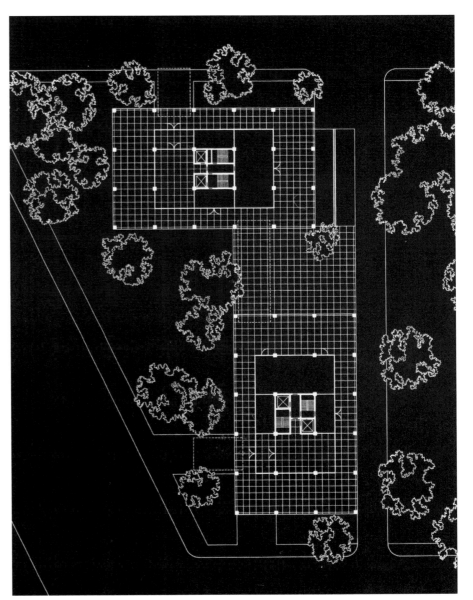

Figure 04
Mies van der Rohe, Lake Shore Drive Apartments, Ground Floor Plan (based on a drawing from Werner Blaser's book of the same name, Birkhäuser - publishers for architecture, 1999).

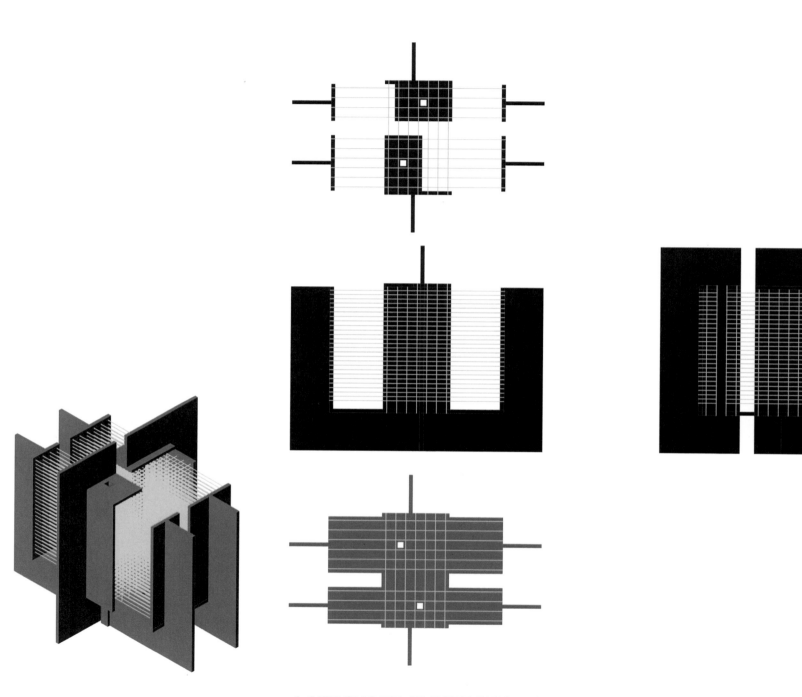

LAKE SHORE, ELECTRONIC MODEL

LAKE SHORE, UNIVERSE

LAKE SHORE, UNIVERSE, 4 VIEWS

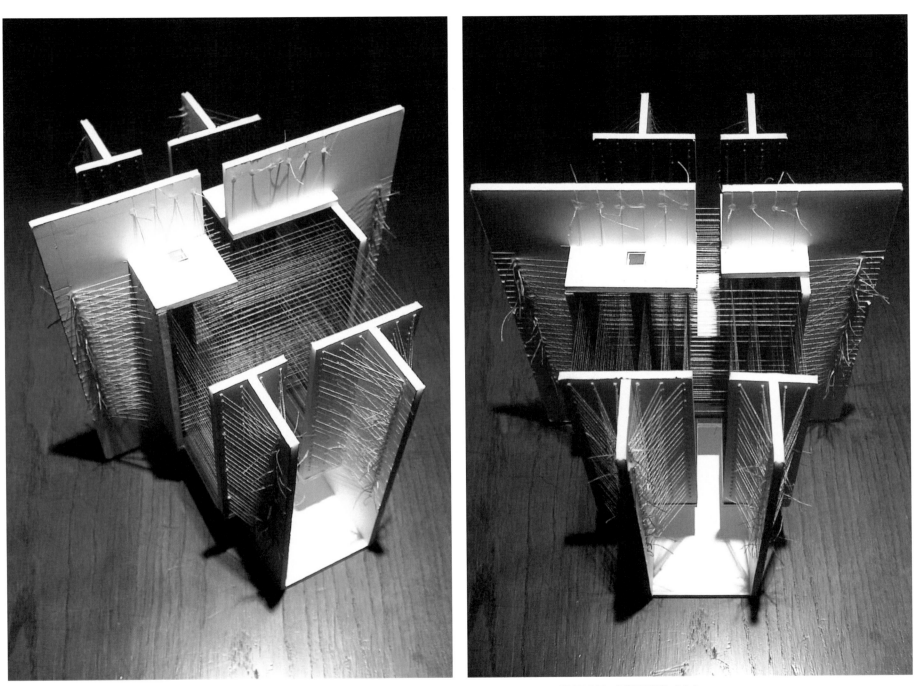

LAKE SHORE, MODEL IN FOAMBOARD & THREAD, VIEWS 1&2

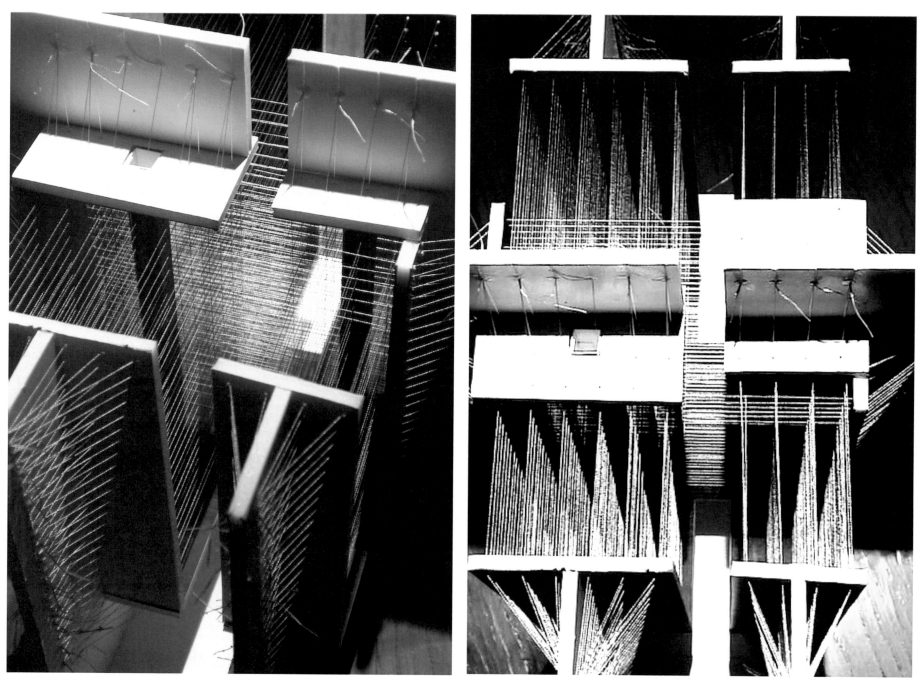

LAKE SHORE, MODEL IN FOAMBOARD & THREAD, VIEWS 3&4

LAKE SHORE, MODEL IN FOAMBOARD & THREAD, VIEWS 5&6

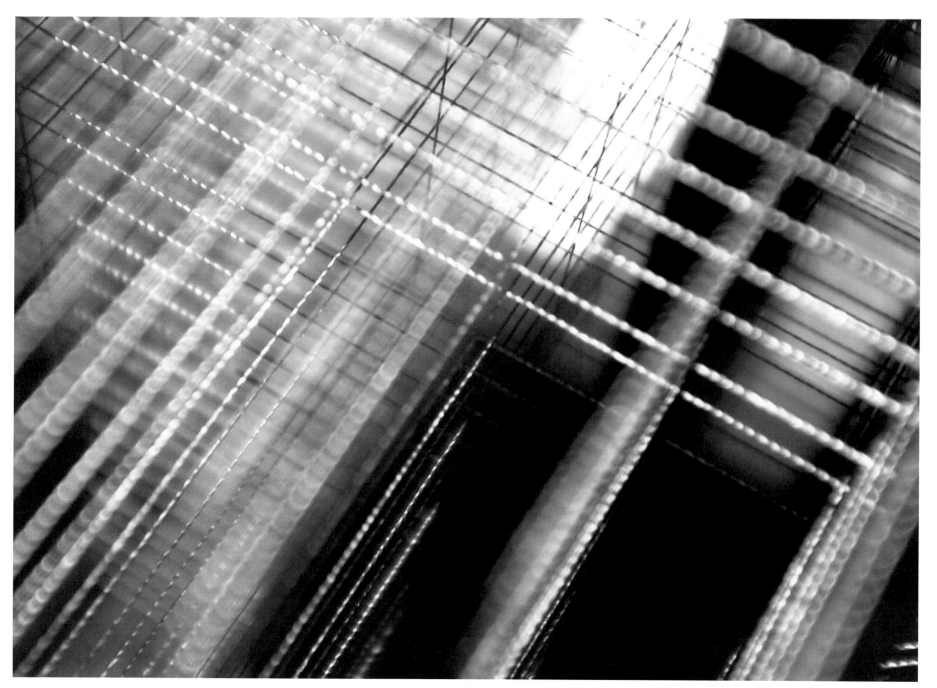

LAKE SHORE, MODEL IN FOAMBOARD & THREAD, DETAIL 1

LAKE SHORE, MODEL IN FOAMBOARD & THREAD, DETAIL 2

Seagram

The second Miesian AIR Grid was based on the design of the Seagram Building, Park Avenue, New York, 1954-'58. The first time they saw the Seagram Building, DWA were struck by the bronze colour, they thought Mies had tinted it that way as a reminder of the Seagram Company's connection to whisky. The Seagram Building was the Seagram Company's American headquarters. It was commissioned by Phyllis Lambert, the daughter of the Seagram Company director Samuel Bronfman and designed by Mies in association with Philip Johnson, the same Johnson who had curated and authored the exhibition and book mentioned in the Introduction, (see p5 above). The Seagram Building set the precedent for the architectural type of the combined office tower and open plaza in New York City and was copied in other cities all around the world. In New York it triggered changes to the city's zoning by-laws.

The chain of events leading to the procurement of the Seagram Building began as early as 1857, with the founding of a distillery in Waterloo, Ontario, Canada. Joseph E. Seagram became a partner in 1869 and sole owner in 1883, giving his name to the company. In 1928, nine years after Joseph's death, his heir, Edward F. Seagram, sold the company to Distillers Corporation Limited, a Montreal-based company founded by Samuel Bronfman and his brothers. The merged company kept the Seagram name. In 1923, during the period of the United States prohibition on the production, importation, transportation and sale of alcoholic beverages, the Bronfmans purchased an American distillery plant, shipped it to Canada and re-assembled it in the LaSalle district of Montreal. From there they shipped liquor from Canada to the French controlled collectivity Saint Pierre and Miquelon, the liquor was then shipped by bootleggers to Rum rows in New York, Jersey and other American states. When prohibition ended, in 1933, the Seagram company was well prepared with an ample stock of aged whiskies, ready to sell on the newly opened American market. At around that time, Seagram set up a company headquarters in the United States and paid a fine of $1.5 million to the US government as settlement for their illegal exporting activities during the time of prohibition - the government had originally asked for $60 million!

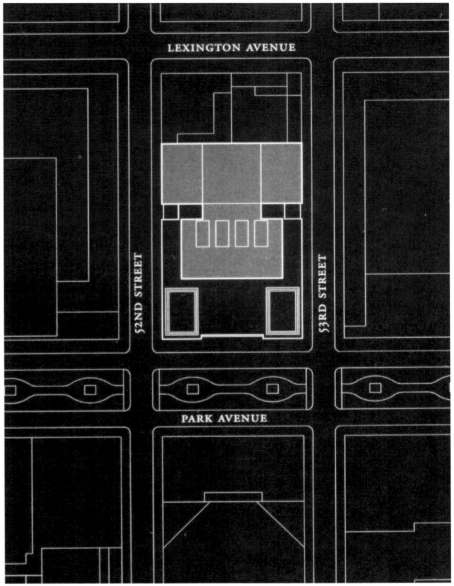

Figure 05

Mies van der Rohe, Seagram Building, Site Plan (from a drawing in Ezra Stoller's book: The Seagram Building, Building Block Series, Princeton Architectural Press, New York, 1999).

23

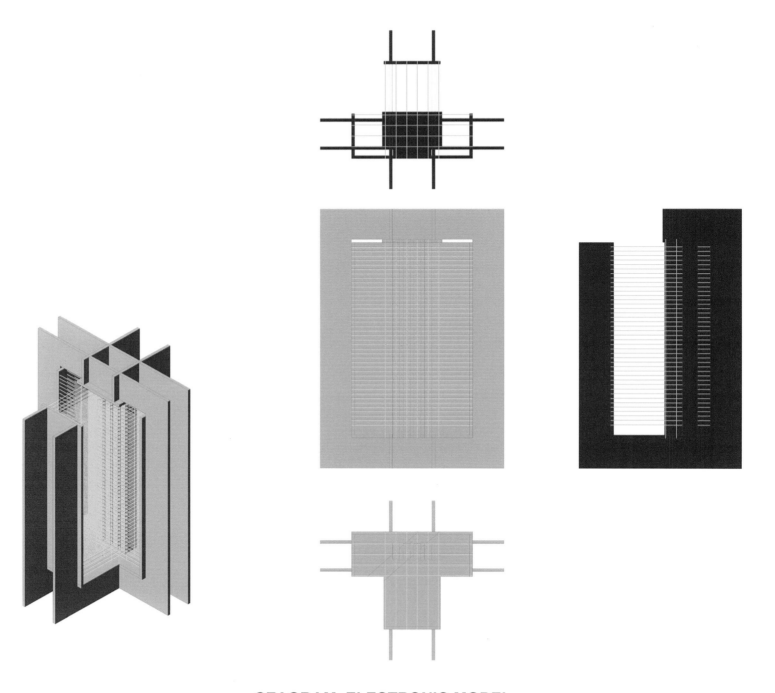

SEAGRAM, ELECTRONIC MODEL

SEAGRAM, UNIVERSE

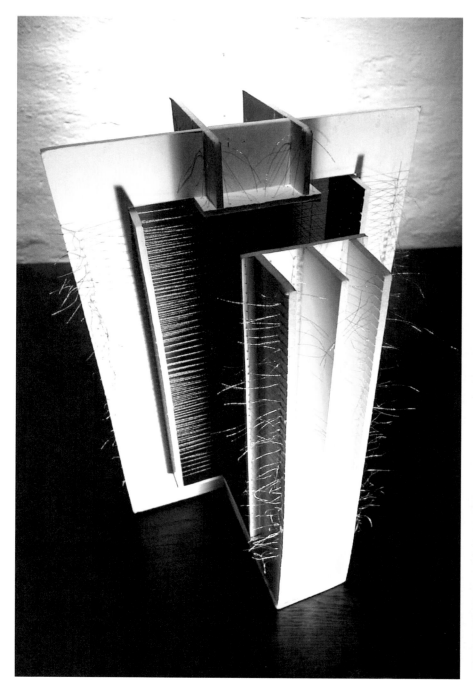

SEAGRAM, MODEL, IN FOAMBOARD & THREAD VIEWS 1&2

SEAGRAM, MODEL IN FOAMBOARD & THREAD VIEWS 3&4

SEAGRAM, MODEL IN FOAMBOARD & THREAD VIEWS 5&6

SEAGRAM, MODEL IN FOAMBOARD & THREAD, VIEWS 7&8

Grenades

In his essay *Notes on Sculpture,* first published in 1966, the artist Robert Morris noted how a simple form, such as a cube, *'accelerates the valence of intimacy as its size decreases from that of one's own body. This is true even if the surface, material and colour are held constant. In fact it is just these properties of surface, color, material, that get magnified into details as the size is reduced. Properties that are not read as detail in large works become details in small works.'* For Morris, intimacy was something to be avoided, because it puts relationships into the artwork, whereas he wanted them taken out, reducing the artwork to *'a function of space, light, and the viewer's field of vision.'***

In order to explore questions of AIR Grid and intimacy, DWA invented a new AIR Grid typology called 'Grenade.' An AIR Grid Grenade is held within a support frame occupying a 9.9 x 9.9 x 9.9 centimetre cubic volume of space. The lattice inside is sewn on a 0.9 or a 0.45 centimetre module. The resultant Grid is good-to-hold-in-the-hand and looking inside is curiously compelling, especially so for the structures sewn on the smaller, 0.45 centimetre module. The special feeling that goes with experiencing an AIR Grid Grenade is a species of 'intimacy,' in Morris' sense. The person who experiences the Grenade must hold the support structure in their hand, as they look at the Grid inside, thus conflating optic and tactile perceptions. The feeling of the relatively small support structure, cupped in their hand, merges with the coloured lines of the tiny infinity inside, it is this combination of containment and extension that prompts the feeling of intimacy.

References:

Robert **Morris**, 'Notes on Sculpture 1-3,' Charles Harrison & Paul Woods (eds), *Art in Theory, 1900-1990, An Anthology of Changing Ideas*, Blackwell, Oxford UK & Cambridge USA, 1992, 813-822

* Morris, 817-818
** Morris, 818 (the minimalist critique of intimacy arose in the 1960s from a concern at the time to find new art forms, adequate to everyday urban experience in a mass production world).

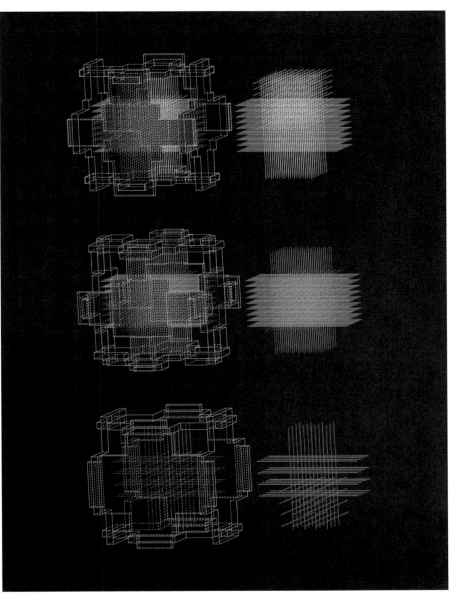

Figure 06

DWA, Grenade Studies, Electronic Models, three species of 9.9 centimetre grenade, from top to bottom: orange/green; blue/pale yellow (0.45 centimetre grid) & red/cyan (0.9 centimetre grid).

FOUR GRENADES ON A WELL-POLISHED FLOOR

GRENADE, FIERY INTERIOR

Schopenhauer

As they looked more closely at the relationship between Mies and Malevich, DWA began to question the sources of Mies' strategies of reduction. They knew, from their reading of biographical texts that Mies owned a complete works of Arthur Schopenhauer.*

In his speculations about the ground of possibility of existence, Schopenhauer argued: the essential purpose of art is to reveal the antagonistic forces that underpin the natural world. He called these 'Ideas,' however, it is important to note, Schopenhauer's Ideas are not Platonic Ideas. Schopenhauer's Ideas are not immaterial forms but sensed realities, which are manifested through psycho-physiological processes that take place in the interactions of a living body with its environment. DWA thought that Mies must have been aware of Schopenhauer's notion of the body as a kind of device for sensing and processing environmental information and they began to understand the forms and spaces Mies designed as evidence of that interest.

The fact that DWA had intuitively grasped this aspect of Mies' thinking, even before studying Schopenhauer, is given in the records of two montage boards that were made around the same time they created Ochenrada and Ochenrad.** The boards were called *Limbo Body* and *Mies Curtain*, they were A1 size, made from ink jet, cardboard, coloured card, tracing paper, pencil and ink.

References:
Werner **Blaser**, *Mies van der Rohe, Continuing the Chicago School of Architecture*, Second Edition, Birkhäuser Verlag.

* In the expanded version of his book *Mies van der Rohe, Lehre und Schule*, Werner Blaser includes some comments about the books Mies' owned. He speculates about which ones were most important to Mies and includes an appendix listing many of those he thought must have been his favourites. The list includes a complete works of Arthur Schopenhauer.
** See Firsts, above

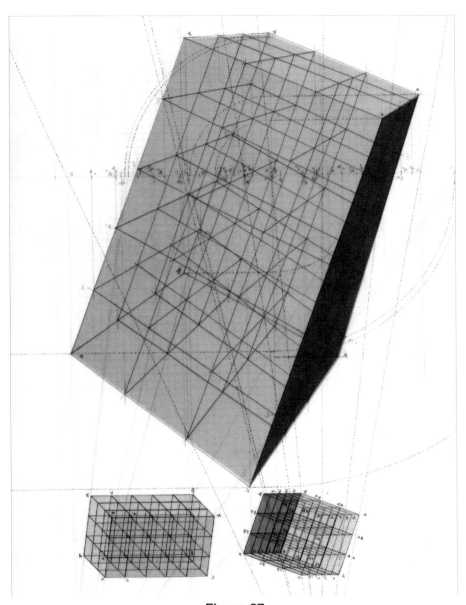

Figure 07
DWA, Architecture as sculpted atmosphere, ink and blue film on tracing paper

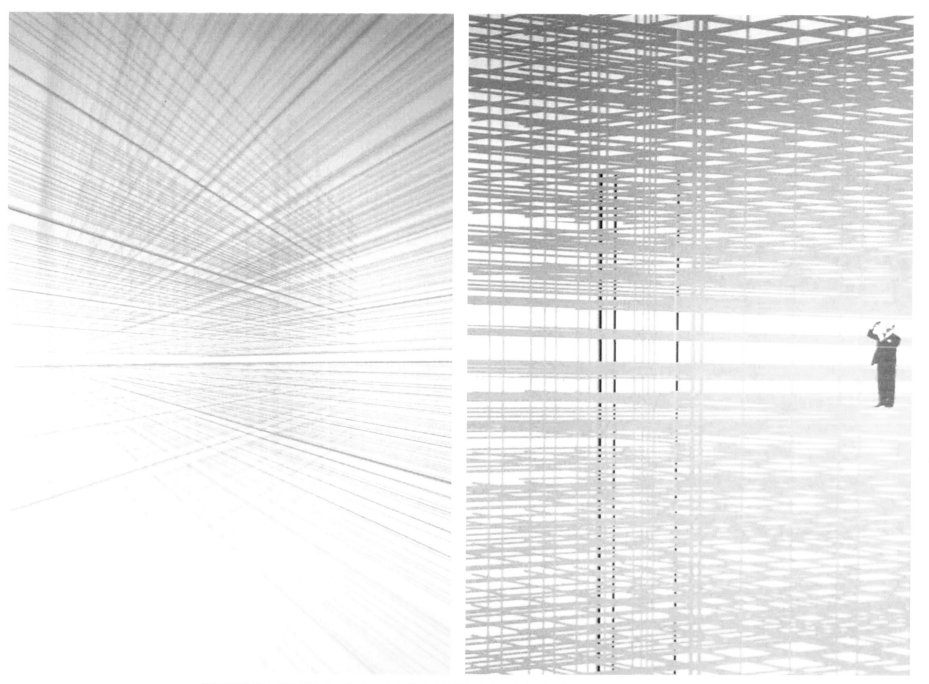

PREPARATORY LAYER: LEFT, LIMBO BODY; RIGHT, MIES CURTAIN

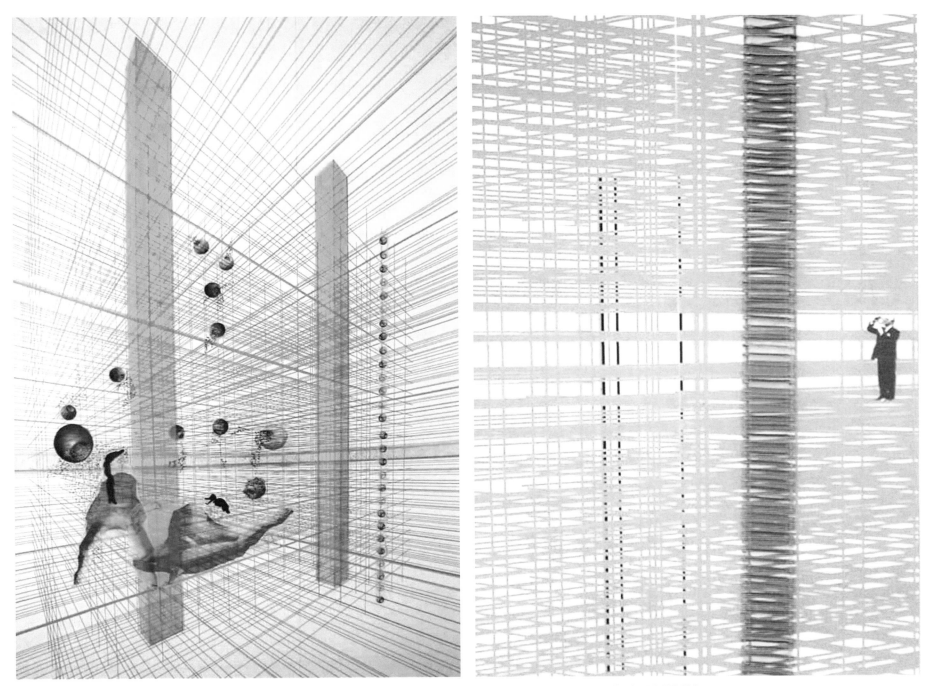

FINAL BOARDS: LEFT, LIMBO BODY; RIGHT, MIES CURTAIN

Turrell

At the time DWA began making AIR Grids, there was something of a craze, especially amongst young architects, for the work of James Turrell. Just like Malevich, Turrell wanted to make art without objects, except, unlike Malevich, who worked with canvas and paint, Turrell experimented with the possibilities of using light to produce artworks.

DWA became interested in a series of Turrell's works called Cross-Corner Projections. He made them by projecting bright light onto two adjacent flat walls, but that is not how the artwork appeared to human viewers. In perception, the Cross-Corner Projections looked like three-dimensional, luminous volumes, hanging suspended in the air (see figure 08). As one critic observed, the three-dimensional impression given by the light *'is enhanced by the fact that it seems to shift in space as the viewer moves back and forth in front of it.'* DWA were beginning to notice something similar, if not exactly the same, with their own AIR Grids. In the more densely sewn Grids, the matrix of threads forming the lattice body would appear to switch on and off, as if responding to the levels of attention given by the viewer.

To test the possibilities of connecting their Grids to Turrell's object-less art, DWA devised a means of sewing an AIR Grid into a corner. Like a Turrell projection, the corner consisted of two flat planes, with cut-out openings, forming and framing a pocket-space behind, where the Grid was sewn. Although it was modelled on a Turrell Cross-Corner Projection, the actual embodied experience of looking at an AIR Grid corner piece was different.

From their experiment, DWA concluded: AIR Grid does not engage the senses in the same way as a Turrell projection piece. The reason is primarily because the material texture of an AIR Grid is more diversified than the homogenous, coloured light that Turrell works with.

References:
Craig **Adcock**, James Turrell, *The Art of Light and Space*, University of California Press, Berkley & Los Angeles, California, 1990
* Adcock, 8

Figure 08
James Turrell, Afrum Red, 1968, Xenon projector changed to MRI wire (based on an image in the exhibition catalogue from the show at the Valencia Museum of Modern Art, 2004 - 2005)

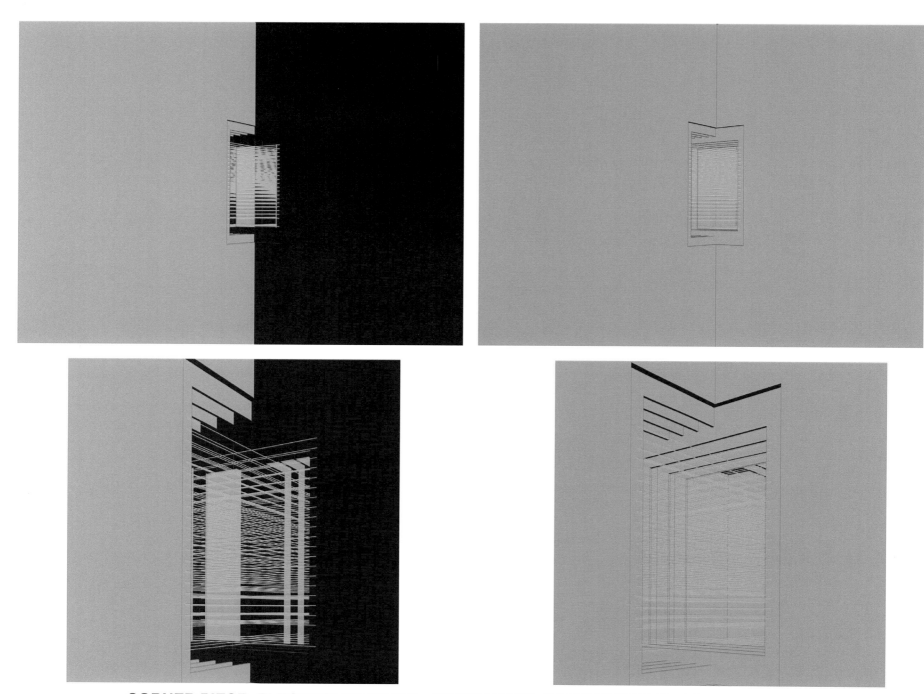

CORNER PIECE, ELECTRONIC MODEL: SOUTH EAST, SOUTH WEST (CLOSE-UP BELOW)

CORNER PIECE, ELECTRONIC MODEL: NORTH WEST, NORTH EAST (CLOSE-UP BELOW)

Whitewall

Since the preoccupations of artists seemed to be influencing what they did, DWA began to question what is it that artists do? They asked: how does the artist's activity differ from that of the architect?

At the time these questions seemed pertinent, DWA was invited to participate in a 'group show' at a studio-gallery in Fashion Street, in the Shoreditch area of London. The studio-gallery owner was interested in DWA's turn to the AIR Grid and wanted to support their inquiry. The owner had recently built a free-standing screen (painted white), inside the studio-gallery space, thereby dividing the space in two. This meant the space could double-up, sometimes functioning as a place of work, on other occasions as a place of display. In display mode the space was called 'Whitewall' and it was as a participant in a Whitewall event that DWA had been invited to the gallery, of course they accepted.

DWA were naive about the institution of art, certainly they were not aware of the complex relationships involved in the making and the showing of art. Nor were they aware of the extent to which what counts as art is determined by those relationships. For DWA, what mattered was the spatial possibilities inherent in the prospect of installing AIR Grid in the proximity of the Whitewall free-standing screen, specifically they were interested in how an Air Grid would appear in that location.

For the Whitewall event, DWA made two new Miesian AIR Grids, one called Marilyn the other Chrystophene. The former, a model of one of Mies' tower designs for Westmount Square in Montreal, Canada, was sewn into a black frame, her threads in shades of red, pink and white. The latter, a 1/200 model of the Seagram building, was sewn into a black frame with threads in shades of green, gold and silver. Marilyn was designed to hang in front of the Whitewall screen, supported by brackets from above. Chrystophene on the other hand, was designed to be embedded in a dark, pocket-space, built to one side of the screen, a kind of artificial corner, from which she would look out, gazing back at any of the Whitewall visitors who happened to be looking at her.

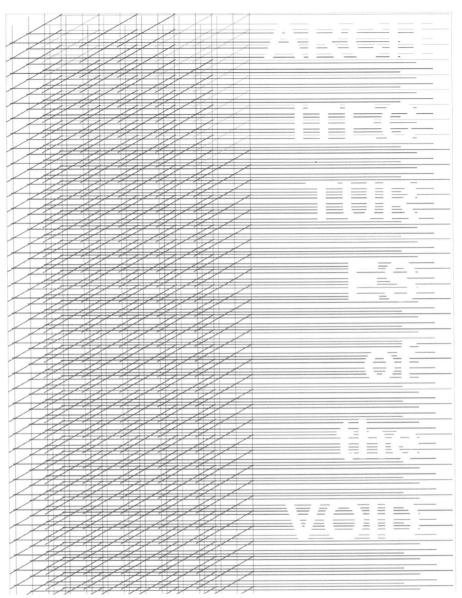

Figure 09

DWA, Whitewall, Air GRID Installation, Fashion Street, Shoreditch, front cover of the invitation card with view of electronic Chrystophene and experimental lettering

MARILYN, ELECTRONIC MODEL: HANGING IN-FRONT OF THE SCREEN

CHRYSTOPHENE, ELECTRONIC MODEL: EMBEDDED TO-ONE-SIDE OF THE SCREEN

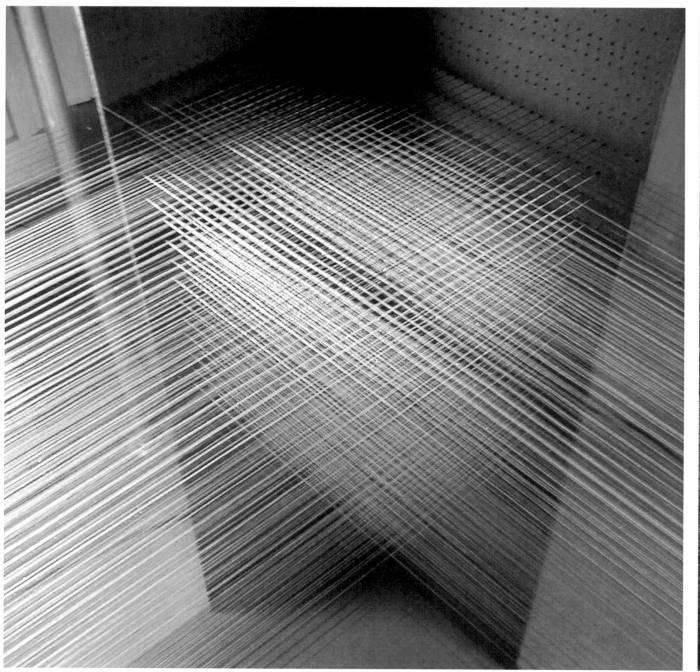

MARILYN, IN THE PROCESS OF MAKING, 2 VIEWS

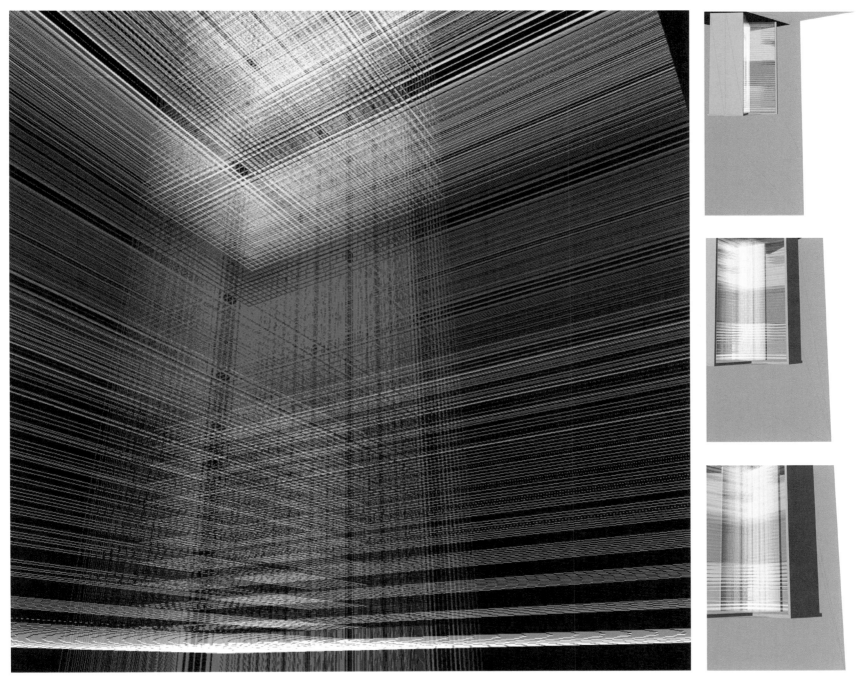

MARILYN, ELECTRONIC MODEL, 4 VIEWS

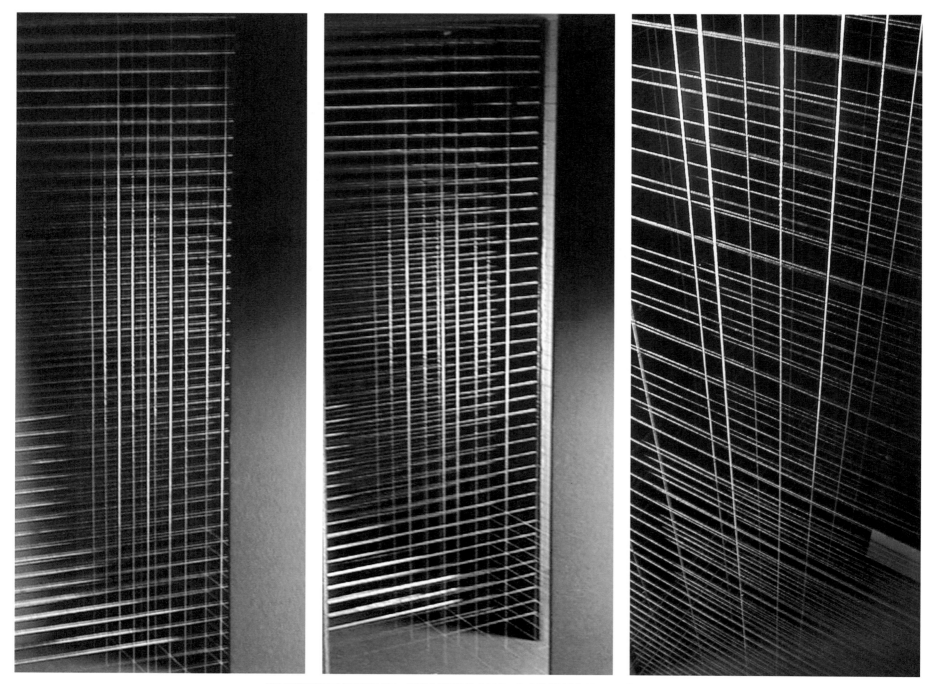

CHRYSTOPHENE, FOAMBOARD & THREAD, 3 VIEWS

CHRYSTOPHENE, ELECTRONIC MODEL, 3 VIEWS

Pareidolia

As a relief from the repetitive lines and right-angles involved in the design and making of AIR Grid, DWA occasionally indulged in a more painterly form of experimentation, based on what they called 'dry painting.'

A dry painting is made by spreading tiny amounts of material - salt crystals, dry pigments and filaments of embroidery thread - between two sheets of transparent film and compacting the sandwich with a rolling pin. The resultant 'painting' is then digitally recorded, either with a flat-bed scanner or by holding it up against a window, or wall, and photographing it with a digital camera. The digital image is then scrutinised by eye and, if it is thought to be of value, stored in the computer. The physical painting is then thrown away.

The process reverses the classical relationship of original and copy - the one that Walter Benjamin theorised in his essay about art works and mechanical reproduction - because, with dry painting, it is the copy and not the original that is valued.

What was especially interesting about the dry painting process was the decision, made at the time of visual scrutiny, whether to keep or to trash the digital image. Although they could never be absolutely certain, DWA could detect a theme running through their decision to keep some images and throw away others. They never could work out what the theme was, but the dry painting process did remind them of Leonardo da Vinci's method for inventing landscape scenes, by looking at a stain-splashed wall as a means of stimulating the imagination. The technique is sometimes known as pareidolia.

References:
Walter **Benjamin**, 'The Work of Art in the Age of Mechanical Reproduction,' *Illuminations*, Harry Zohn (trans.), 1969, 221-4
Hubert **Damisch**, A Theory of /Cloud/ Toward a History of Painting, Stanford University Press, California, 2002

* Damisch, 32-35

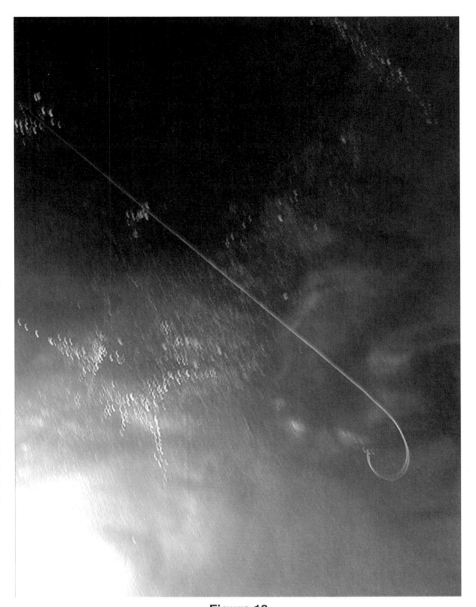

Figure 10

DWA, Dry Painting, visualisation of a digital image file (this one looks like a fish-hook shaped tendril floating in an oily fluidic substance with a life-form reaching up to snatch it from below)

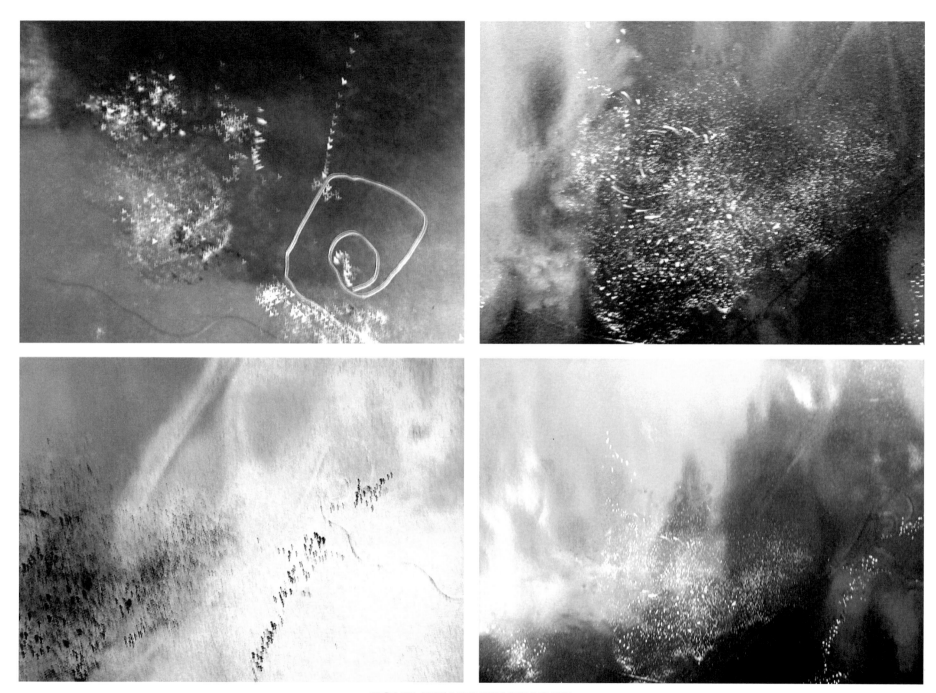

FOUR DRY PAINT IMAGES

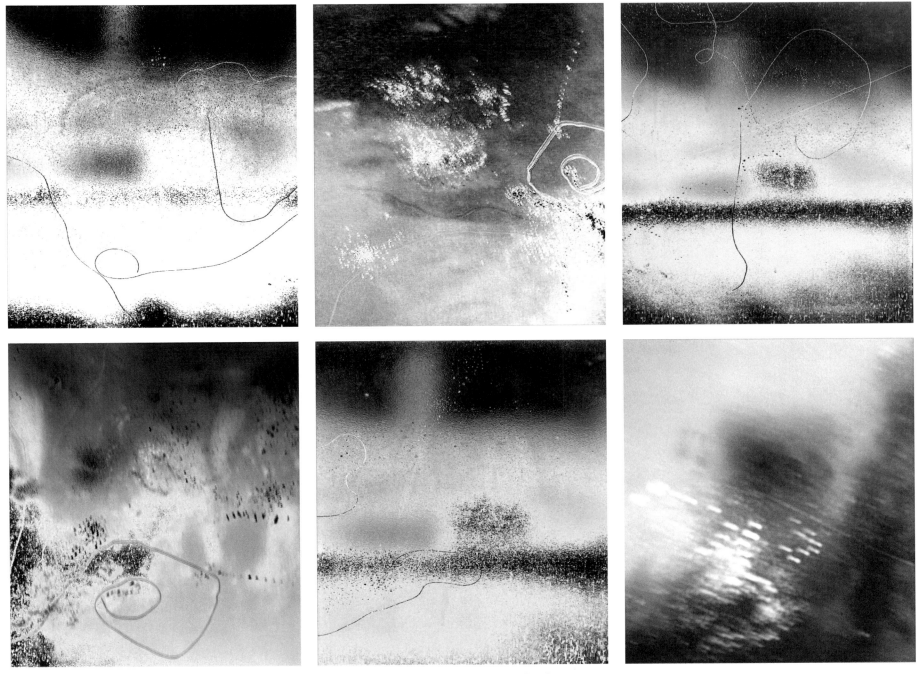

SIX DRY PAINT IMAGES

NNG 01

Having visited Mies' New National Gallery in Berlin, DWA began to speculate about the possibilities of using it as a location for installing a number of bespoke AIR Grid structures. To this end they surveyed and analysed the Gallery very carefully, revisiting it several times and put together a set of drawings, describing the building as it was and as it might be, if it became a home for AIR Grid. As part of their work process, DWA researched the history of the Gallery and in so doing they came across a story about the raising of the enormous black-grid roof-form that hovers above the surface of the podium as though it were weightless.

The roof-grid was constructed in sections on the podium surface, welded together and then raised, as a single piece, by eight hydraulic jacks. The jacks were placed at the points along the perimeter, coinciding with the location of the eight cruciform columns that would replace them once the roof-grid was in position. In his biography, Franz Schulze recounts how Mies, who had watched patiently for nine hours throughout the assembly and raising of the roof-grid, had himself driven up and onto the podium in a Mercedes, where he proceeded, first, to thank the builders for their efforts and second, to comment on how amazed he had been when the roof-grid *'raised itself up without a sound.'* *

DWA were familiar with the myths that had built up around Mies, where the architect's association with 'silence' had become something of a cliché. And so, to find the source of the myth in something Mies' had actually said while witnessing a physical act of building had a profound effect on them. Immediately, all the confused, idealist readings of Mies flew from their minds and, from that moment, things started to clarify as they realised it was this materialist Mies that mattered most to the AIR Grid project.

References:

Franz **Schulze**, *Mies van der Rohe, A Critical Biography,* University of Chicago Press, Chicago and London, 1985, 303-311

*Schulze, 303-311

Figure 11
DWA Archives, A Visit to the New National Gallery, with two portable AIR Grid structures resting on the podium, roof-grid above, columns and glass-screen in the zone of separation

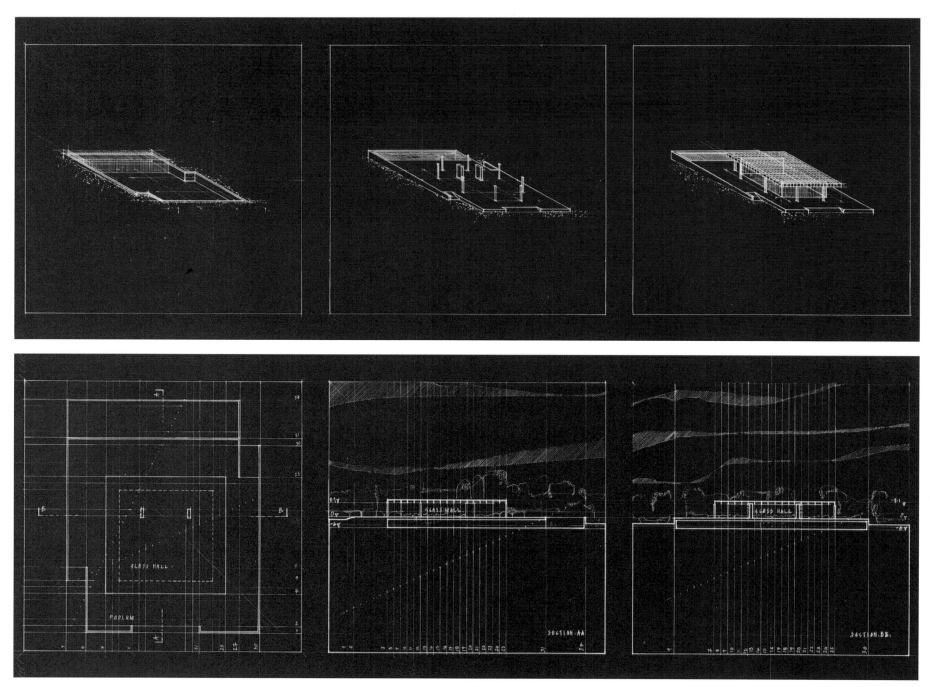

SURVEY & ANALYSIS DRAWINGS 1

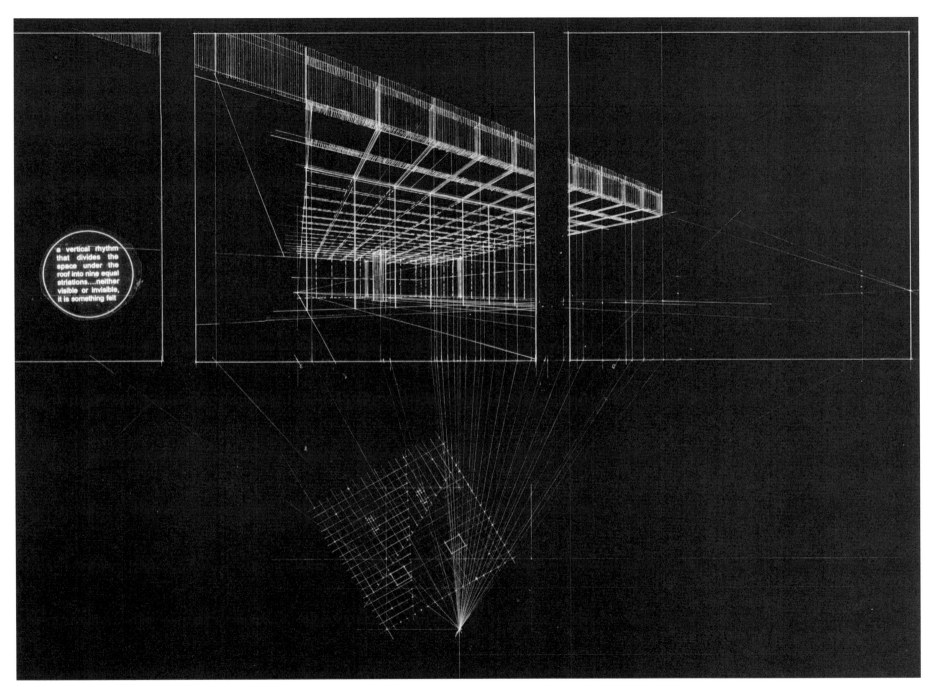

a vertical rhythm that divides the space under the roof into nine equal striations....neither visible or invisible, it is something felt

SURVEY & ANALYSIS DRAWINGS 2

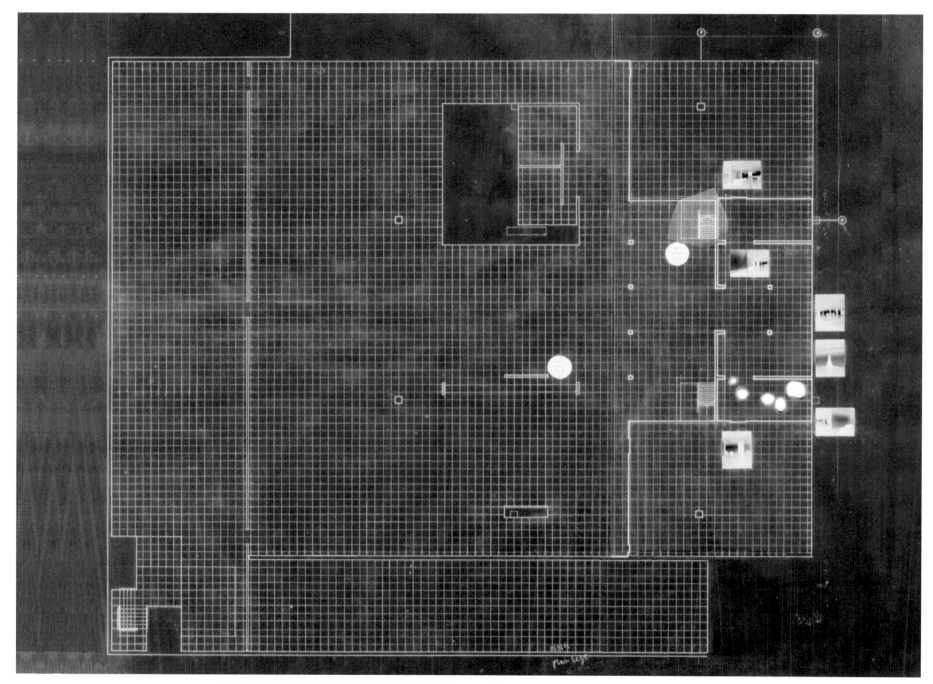

PROPOSAL FOR A SERIES OF AIR GRID INSTALLATIONS, PLAN

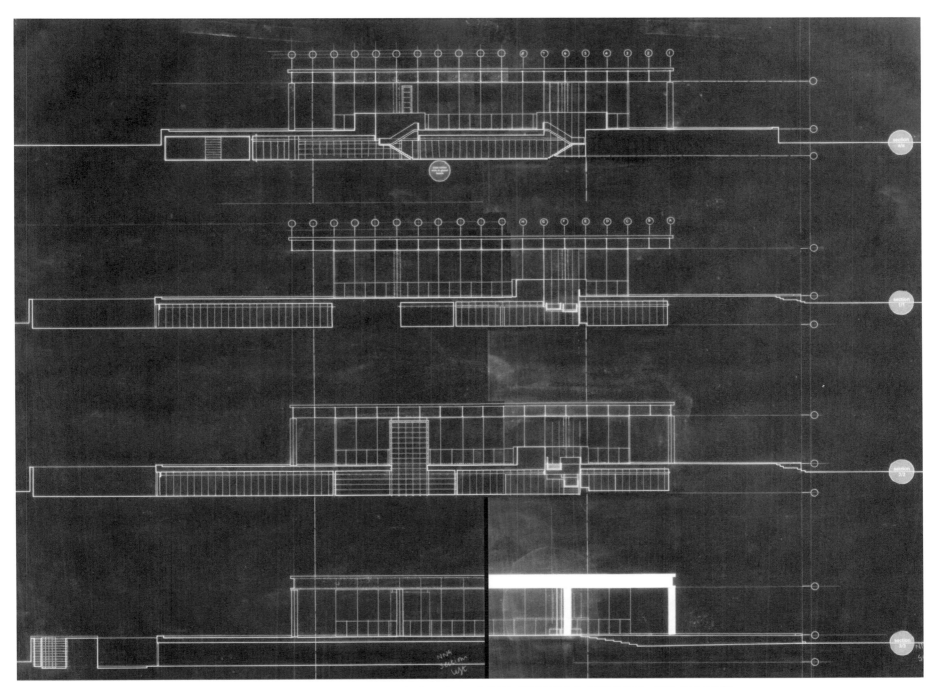

PROPOSAL FOR A SERIES OF AIR GRID INSTALLATIONS, SECTIONS

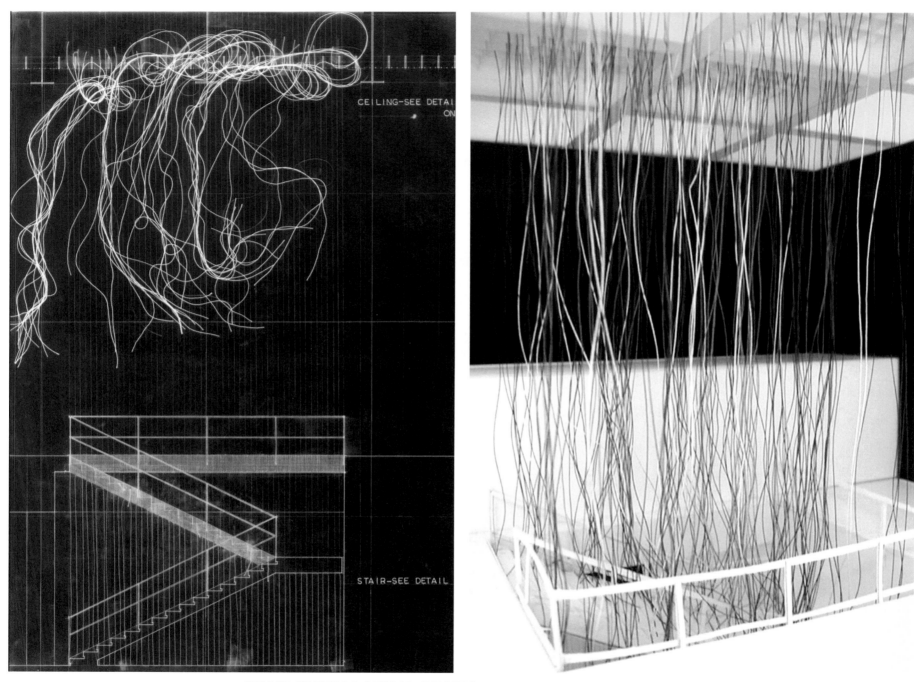

CEILING-SEE DETAIL
ON

STAIR-SEE DETAIL

STAIR INSTALLATION, SECTION & VIEW OF THE MODEL

STAIR INSTALLATION, VIEWS OF THE MODEL & DETAIL

STAIR INSTALLATION, VIEWS OF THE MODEL

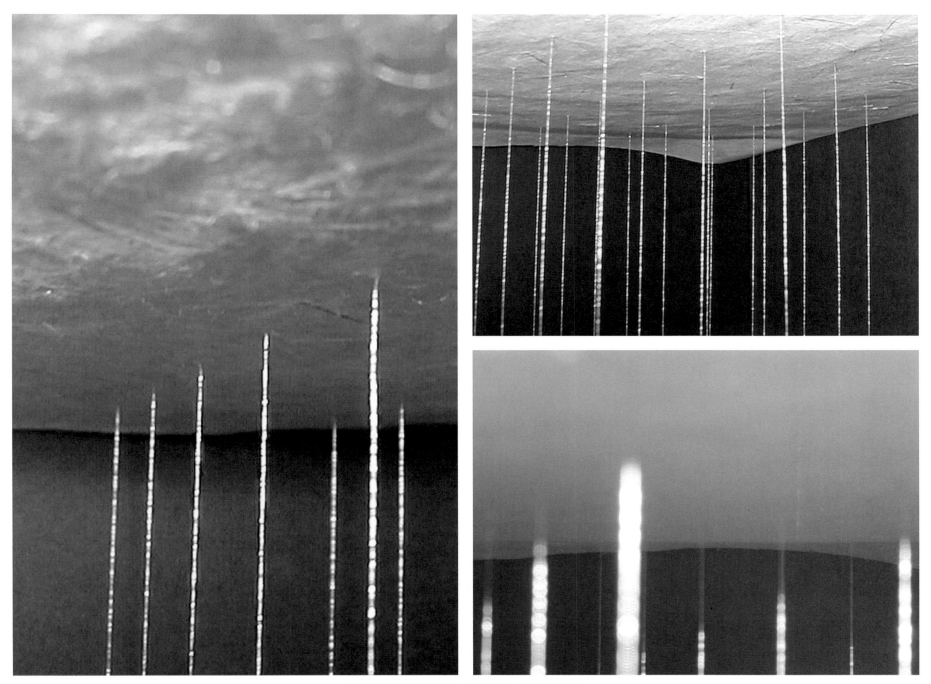

STAIR INSTALLATION, DETAILS

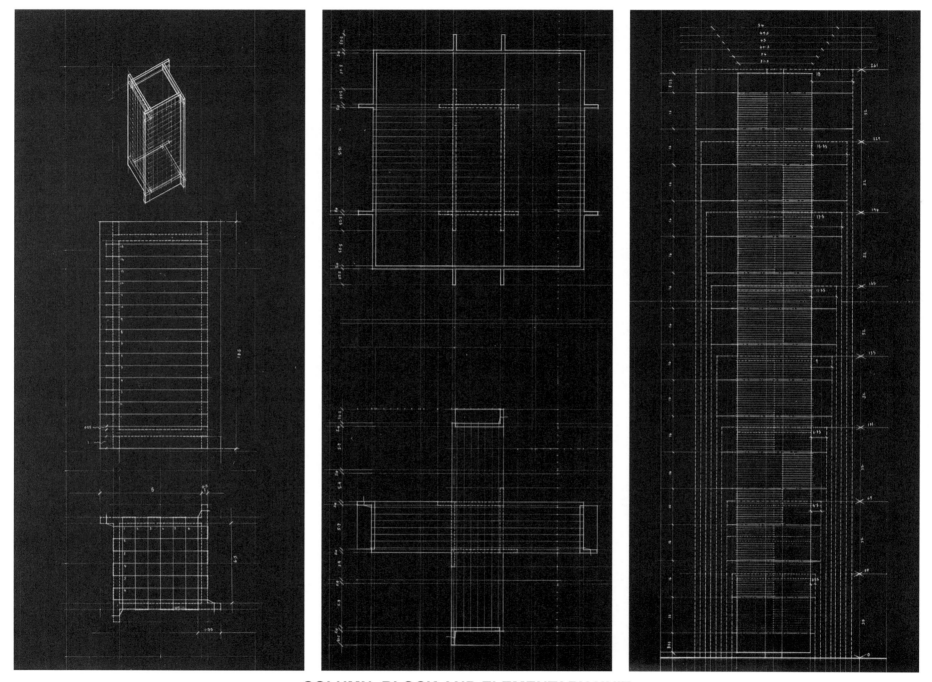

COLUMN, BLOCK AND ELEMENTARY UNIT

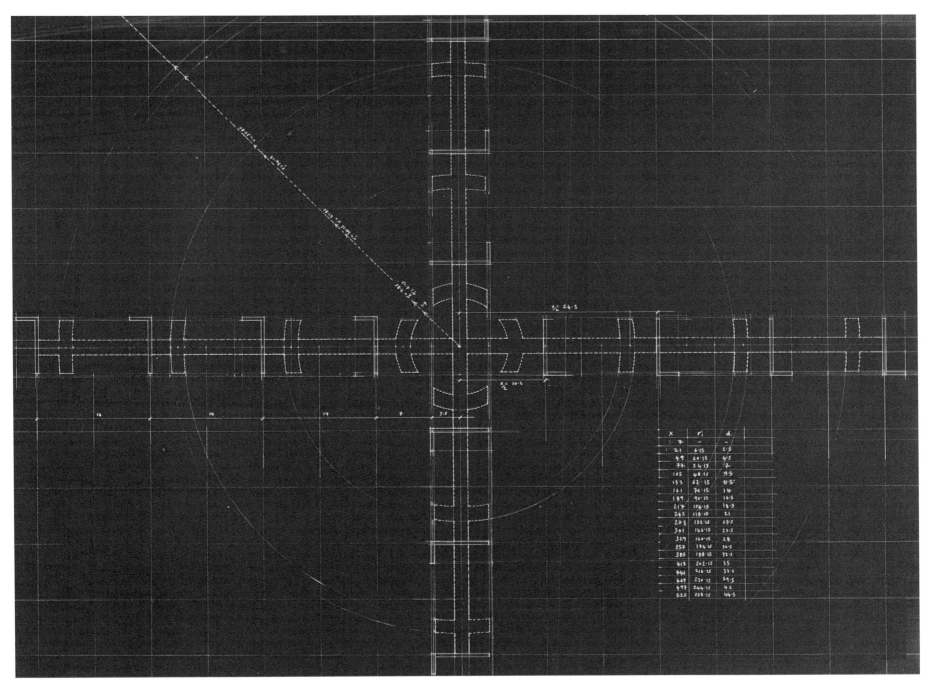

EXTENSION DIAGRAM

Poetic Structures

At around the same time they began to look at the New National Gallery, DWA set aside time to design a collection of new AIR Grid structures, based on the size of play-forms often found in parks and gardens, with names like Play Tower, Jungle Gym and Swing Set. Although the AIR Grid structures imitated the size and scale of active play-forms, they were not intended to excite the desires of the people who engaged with them in quite the same way.

To understand the new AIR Grid structures we need to turn to the writings of the 18th century architect, archeologist and theorist, Julien-David Le Roy and to his notion of 'poetic architecture.' To explain what he meant by poetic architecture, Le Roy asked his readers to imagine two different types of spatial boundary, first a richly decorated wall and second an open colonnade. He points out: because it is a solid barrier in space, it is impossible for a human being to actually get inside the wall, but they can contemplate the beauty of the wall from a distance. On the other hand, the colonnade, thanks to its openness, actually invites the human being to physically enter it and to move about inside.

Le Roy likened the experience of the decorated wall to that of viewing a painting and he referred to the kinds of structures that promote this kind of experience by the term 'painterly architecture.' On the other hand, he likened the more immersive mode of experience, associated with the colonnade, to listening to poetry. And he referred to the kinds of open-form structures that encourage this kind of immersive experience 'poetic architecture.'

The new AIR Grid structures were intended to be poetic in Le Roy's sense, i.e., not because they refer to the content of a poem but because they invite people to engage with them by moving around amongst them.

Figure 12
AIR Grid Poetic Structure, Field of Ten, Configuration A, View 6 of 9

References:
Julien-David **Le Roy**, *The Ruins of the Most Beautiful Monuments of Greece,* Getty Publications, Los Angeles, 2004

FIELD OF TEN, CONFIGURATION A, VIEW LEFT TO RIGHT

FIELD OF TEN, CONFIGURATION A, VIEW RIGHT TO LEFT

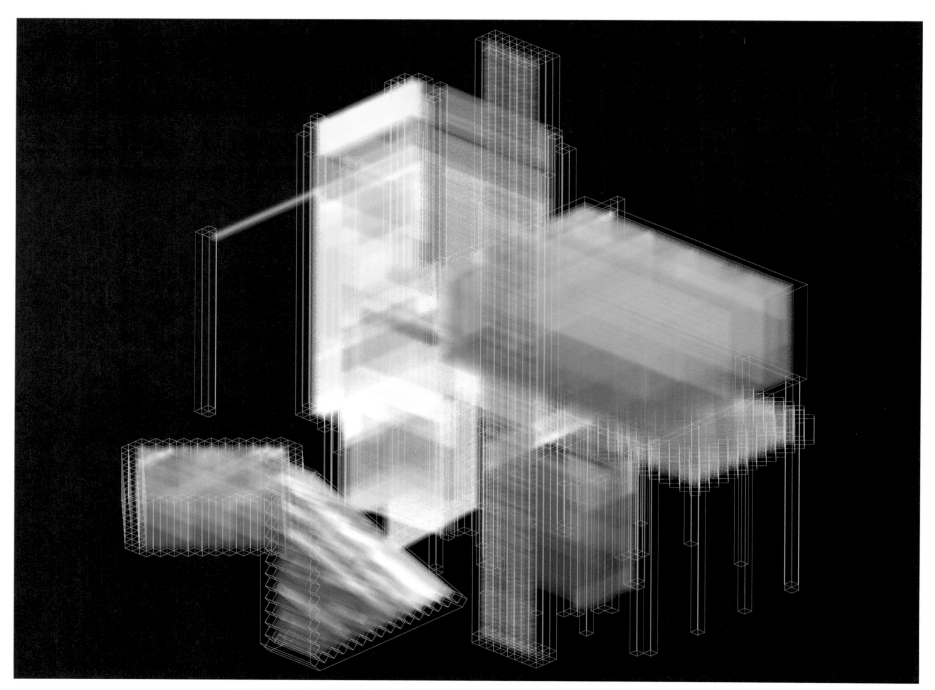

FIELD OF TEN, CONFIGURATION A, AXONOMETRIC VIEW 1

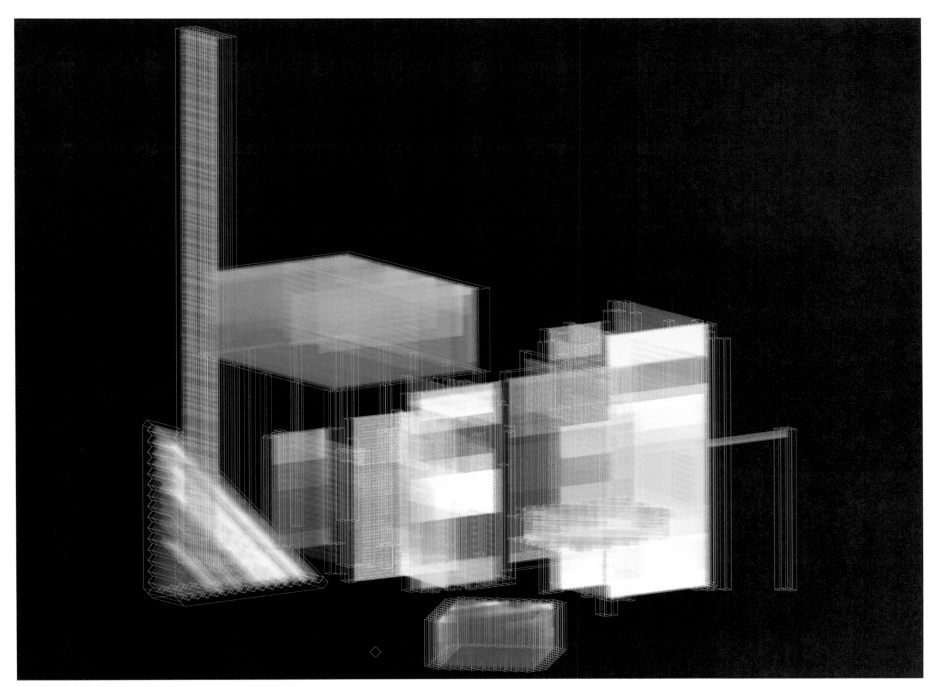

FIELD OF TEN, CONFIGURATION A, AXONOMETRIC VIEW 2

FIELD OF TEN, CONFIGURATION A, VIEWS 1,2,3 & 4 OF 9

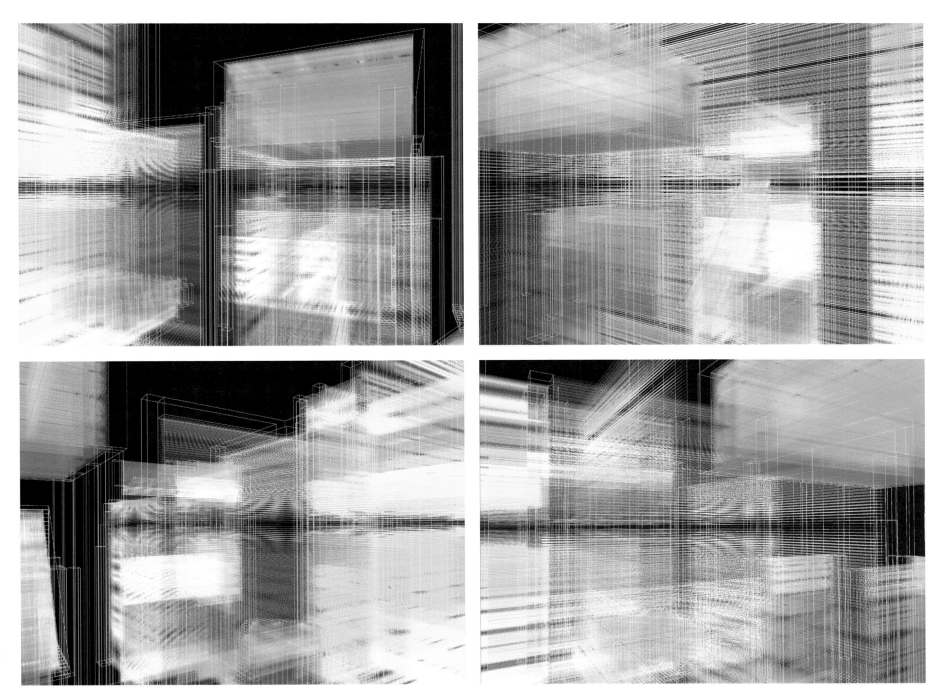

FIELD OF TEN, CONFIGURATION A, VIEWS 5,7,8 & 9 OF 9

Niche Grids

This strand of AIR Grid inquiry asked about the possibility of embedding AIR Grid structures in the pocket spaces that are sometimes found behind the surface lining of a room. Once DWA began to think about this kind of 'negative' space they found their imaginations full of images of secret cupboards, niches, passages and hidden doorways, but they also thought about mouse holes. They were especially reminded of *The Tale of Two Bad Mice*, written by the British writer, illustrator, natural scientist and conservationist, Beatrix Potter. The book was first published in 1904, it is about two mice who live in the wainscotting of a young girl's nursery. One day the mice leave their mouse hole and venture out into the middle of the nursery, where they come across a brand new dolls house. The mice enter the tiny house but are soon disappointed when they find the dishes of food, lavishly displayed on the dining room table, are actually not food at all but made of plaster. Their disappointment drives the mice into a rage, they smash the plaster dishes and throw the dolls house furniture out the window. Eventually they leave, but not before gathering a number of dolls house curtains and cushions, dragging them away, across the nursery floor and back to the mouse-hole.

Conflating the notion of mice-coming-out-of-the-wainscotting with the four-square image of the dolls house (as illustrated in Potter's book), DWA imagined a new type of AIR Grid and a new AIR Grid narrative. They imagined a type of Grid that would be housed in a niche, formed in the surface lining of a room. The niche Grid would remain silent and still in the daytime, but at night, when no one was around, it would leave the niche and venture out into the room. Unlike Potter's Bad Mice, the niche Grid did not come out to scavenge for food, it came out because it could somehow sense and was attracted to, the relatively open expanse of the room. Once out in the open, the Grid would be able to leap about and shimmer, enjoying the mass, radiance and colour of its own body, leaping about in the moonlight, or, if the sky were overcast, by the light of an artificial moon balloon, programmed to switch on if needed.

References:

Beatrix Potter *The Tale of Two Bad Mice,* London, Fredrick Warne & Co., 1904

Figure 13
Niche Grids, leaping and shimmering in the moonlight

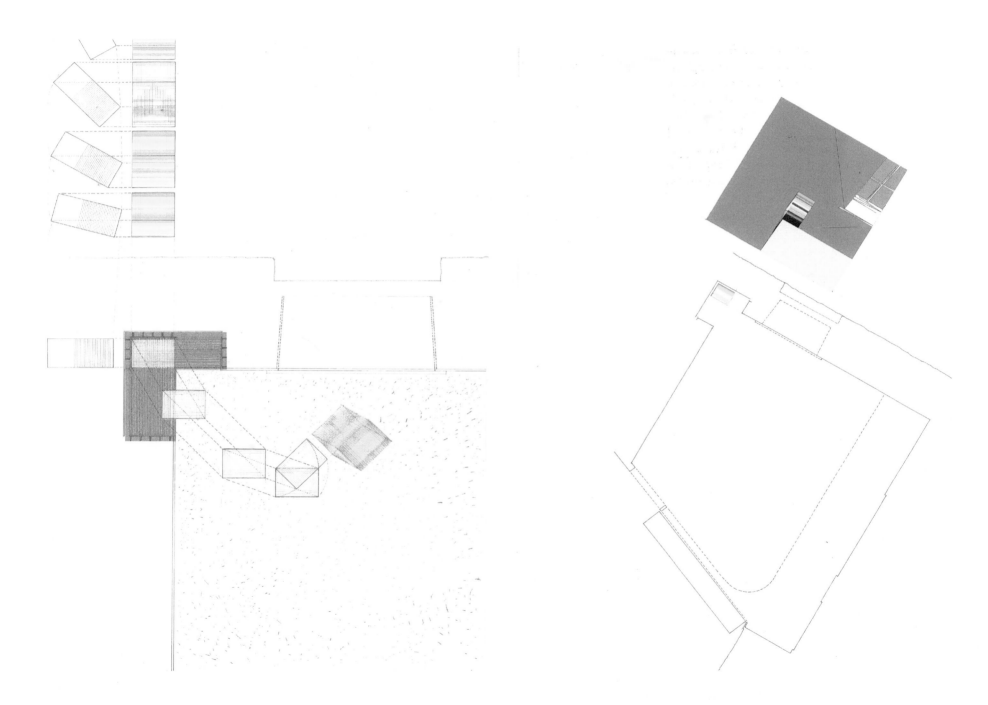

POCKET SPACE, STUDY ONE, SHEET A

POCKET SPACE, STUDY ONE, SHEET B

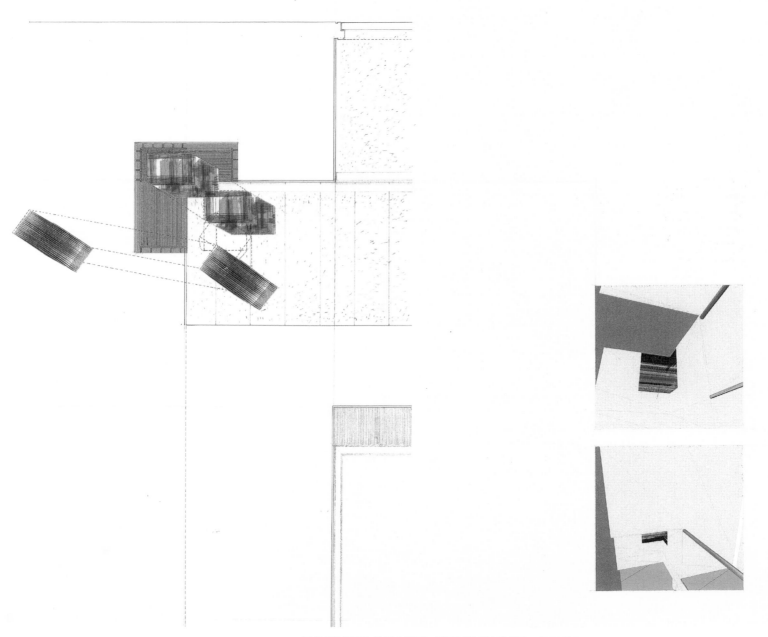

POCKET SPACE, STUDY TWO, SHEET A

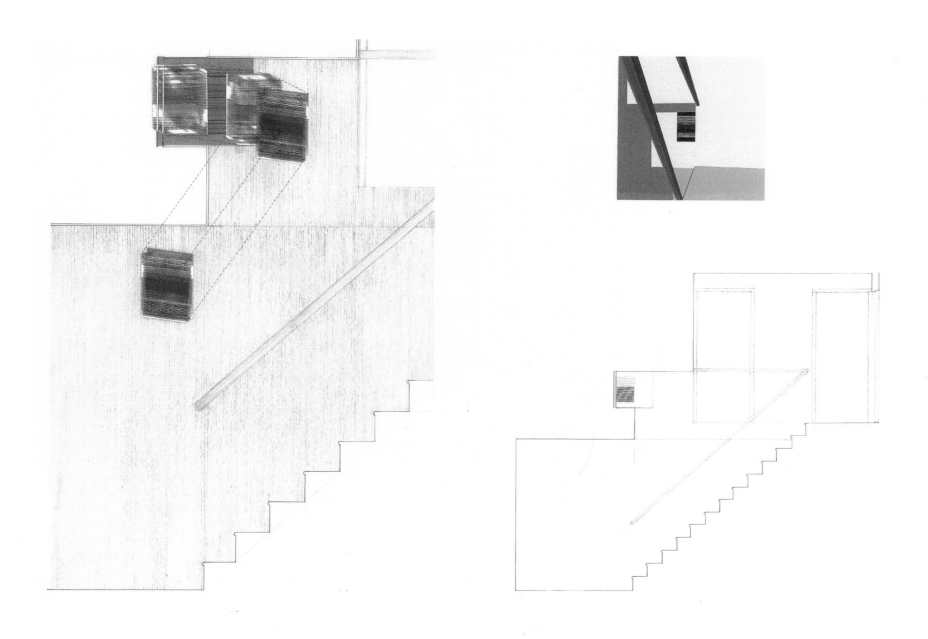

POCKET SPACE, STUDY TWO, SHEET B

Lightning Source UK Ltd.
Milton Keynes UK
UKRC020954200721
387467UK00001B/5

* 9 7 8 0 9 9 2 8 7 6 8 9 0 *